Life Lessons From Leo

Holly Garner

an imprint of Sunbury Press, Inc.
Mechanicsburg, PA USA

For information about special discounts for bulk purchases, please contact Sunbury Press Orders Dept. at (855) 338-8359 or orders@sunburypress.com.

To request one of our authors for speaking engagements or book signings, please contact Sunbury Press Publicity Dept. at publicity@sunburypress.com.

FIRST SPECKLED EGG PRESS EDITION: May 2025

Interior design by Crystal Devine | Cover by Lawrence Knorr / Illustrations coordinated by Katie Cressman | Edited by Katie Cressman.

Publisher's Cataloging-in-Publication Data
Names: Garner, Holly, author.
Title: Life lessons from Leo / Holly Garner.
Description: First trade paperback edition. | Mechanicsburg, PA : Speckled Egg, 2025.
Summary: The world needs more love, more kindness, and more loyalty. The world could use more dogs like Leo. Dogs have a unique way of teaching us valuable lessons—how to love, comfort, and uplift those around us. Leo, an irreplaceable part of our family, shared countless life lessons with us. This book is a reflection of those lessons, ones we will forever hold close to our hearts.
Identifiers: ISBN : 979-8-88819-344-0 (paperback).
Subjects: JUVENILE FICTION / School & Education | JUVENILE FICTION / Family / General | JUVENILE FICTION / Social Themes / Emotion & Feelings.

Designed in the USA
0 1 1 2 3 5 8 13 21 34 55

For the Love of Books!

To my grandson, Hudson–
you are loved and treasured beyond measure.
May you never stop laughing,
loving, and learning.

The world needs more love, more kindness, and more loyalty. The world could use more dogs like Leo.

Dogs have a unique way of teaching us valuable lessons—how to love, comfort, and uplift those around us.

Leo, an irreplaceable part of our family, shared countless life lessons with us. This book is a reflection of those lessons, ones we will forever hold close to our hearts.

LEO

Love Lessons From Leo

Love others fiercely and without judgment.

Find joy in simple pleasures.

Feed your mind with peace, hope, love, and truth. Your mind will believe what you feed it.

Be quick to forgive and admit when you are wrong.

Love Lessons From Leo

When you love, love with your whole heart.

Stay Connected to Home: Even as you move on to new chapters in your life, find ways to stay connected with family and friends.

Things you love are best when shared.

Legacy Lessons From Leo

- Don't be afraid to shake things up.
- Keep trying new things. You never know what you may be best at.
- Volunteer your time and talents in your community.
- Practice patience. The best things in life are worth waiting for.
- Effort is the key to achievement and improvement.

Legacy Lessons From Leo

Believe it is possible and dream until it's true.

Appreciate what you have. Be happy with the little things.

If you are learning a new trick or overcoming an obstacle, be persistent. Do not be afraid of failing a few times!

You have more potential inside you than you realize. Push yourself to be the best you that you can be.

Legacy Lessons From Leo

Logical Lessons From Leo

- Overcome your fears and try new things, even if it means making mistakes.

- Call your mother.

- Focus on Being a Better You: don't compare yourself with others.

- Take a walk every day.

Logical Lesson From Leo

Ask for help. It's a sign of strength, not weakness.

Who you are with is always more important than where you are.

Be mindful of what you post on social media.

Logical Lessons From Leo

Be open to new ideas, opportunities, and challenges.

Don't settle. EVER.

Every decision you make has a consequence that could be good or bad.

Look forward to the future, but enjoy the present.

Loyalty Lessons From Leo

- Protect and defend those you love.

- Be generous. In life, you get what you give.

- Compliment at least 3 people every day.

- Stand up for what you believe, even if you are nervous. Being brave and afraid often happens at the same time.

- Be there when people need you.

Lifting Lessons From Leo

Be the first to say hello.

Surround yourself with people who spread light and sunshine.

Make others feel noticed and appreciated.

Lifting Lessons From Leo

- Be quick to encourage others.
- Look up more. The people and the beauty around you are more important than your phone.
- Greet people warmly at the door.
- Savor every magical moment that life gives you.

- Win with humility. Lose with dignity.

- Keep your eye on the ball. Keep swinging.

- Support your teammates.

- Promise big. Deliver big.

- Always remember to have fun when you play.

Life is a playground

Leadership Lessons From Leo

Leadership Lessons From Leo

Help someone up off the ground if you see them go down.

Be a good sport and play fairly.

Work harder than others expect.

Be coachable.

When you have a passion, give it everything you've got.

As you close this book, remember that the lessons from Leo will never be lost. They will stay in our hearts forever.

The truth is, the best parts of Leo—his love, kindness, and loyalty—can live on in all of us. Just like Leo, we have the power to make the world a brighter, better place, simply by being the best friends and companions we can be.

Let his spirit inspire you every day!

About the Author

Holly Garner has been an educator for over 30 years. Her experience as a teacher, reading specialist, elementary principal, and most importantly, a mom of three boys, helped develop her passion for social emotional learning in schools. Currently, Holly serves as the Director of the Grace B. Luhrs Elementary Lab School and an Associate Professor at Shippensburg University in Pennsylvania. She has written 9 other children's books, including *Letters from Leo*, *More Letters from Leo*, *STUCK*, *The Memory Keeper*, and the Emotion Ensemble series.

In her free time, Holly enjoys playing games with her family, playing pickleball, reading on the beach, and planning parties.

Other Books by Holly Garner

The Emotion Ensemble Series

Why is Angry so Angry?

Why is Sad so Sad?

Why is Frustrated so Frustrated?

Why is Jealous so Jealous?

Why is Lonely so Lonely?

STUCK!

Letters from Leo

More Letters from Leo

www.ingramcontent.com/pod-product-compliance
Lightning Source LLC
Chambersburg PA
CBHW081640040426
42449CB00014B/3393